GW00634116

First published 1999
Text © Graeme Lewis 1999
Illustrations © Matt Tweed 1999

Published by Wooden Books Ltd
Walkmill, Cascob, Presteigne, Powys, Cymru LD8 2NT

British Library Cataloguing in Publication Data
Lewis, G.
Dongarusalem

A CIP catalogue record for this book is
available from the British Library

ISBN 1 902418 13 1

Printed and bound in Britain
by the Cromwell Press,
Trowbridge, Wiltshire, England.

DONGARUSALEM

AND OTHER POEMS

by

Graeme Lewis

with illustrations by

Matt Tweed

Especially for my children Fynnbar & Sibi,
and She whose dark eyes haunt me always.

Many thanks to the Twyford Dongas Tribe and kindred souls
for being there and teaching me, to artist Matt and Colonel
Twiddles for suggesting him, to Pãlo Custeau for inspiring the
poem "Corn Circles", to Anna Don Francesco for inspiring the
illustration on page 15, to David Icke for being a great teacher,
to Michael Glickman for staying true to the Cause, to the
interdimensional (ssh!) Circlemakers, and finally
to my mum Valerie & Fuzzclot the Cat.

CONTENTS

Introduction   1
Corn Circles   2
A Friend from the Stars   8
Dongarusalem   10
The Pentonvilliad   16
Tears of Jonah   22
V.E. No Tree Day   24
Fair-Minded Man   30
The Architects of Annihilation   32
Stay (as Lush Woods should)   38
Time (the Real story)   42
Warszawa Snaps   44
Moongate   48
Prayer to Avalonia   52
Can Orphans Know their Parents?   56
America! I Love You   58

INTRODUCTION

It is currently quite out of fashion to be a poet unless you are a pop musician too. The Oxford University Press recently axed its ancient and unique poetry department because no-one buys poetry any more and, anyway, one gets the feeling with much modern art that we've seen it all before.

The poems in this small millenial edition from the Wooden Books Press do not fit the modern mould and would never normally see publication. They spring from the rare realm of the genuine British living spoken tradition, the world of road-protest camps and passionate green political activity that most of us never see except on our television sets.

As a vicar I find these poems and illustrations interesting, heartening and thought-provoking. How many times have I too secretly hoped that a new chicken-factory would not be permitted or that a favourite hill or valley could be saved from 'development'. After my father was killed in France at the end of the War, I vowed to protect the country I love in every way I could. I truly believe that the young men and women who fight for the old ways and the old trees of this old land would be joined by my father and many like him were they still with us. I commend this volume.

Rev. C. E. Thistlewaite
Upton Bottomley, Wiltshire 1999

CORN CIRCLES

Glastonbury, September 1991

I know there are men in factory farming
  who like to mix up lots of things
Like scales of cats, and chicken wings,
  pig hormones and chrome-plated chromosomes.
These, with a little modified corn flavouring,
  become our daily staple bread,
From a ripe, majestic, full green head,
  crushed down to grow a pinched inch tall
  on tried and tested laboratory stalks.
I know they approve in the House of Lords
  or wherever chemical money talks.

They fence in the corn with wire walls
  to spare any danger to rushing cars
That pass it by on the brittle highways
  holding little tinned people
Who can't afford to stop and sit
  in nature's byways.
I do know they feed it to baby hens
  with debeaked heads and broken wings,
Who spend all day in battery pens
  which some thoughtful farmer
  provides for them.

But I know not much
no, I don't know much
... about corn circles

I do know a million children die
   because they always see a parched brown sky,
And see where dead trees used to ride
   the plains where now the beef cows die,
And walled veal units where the small calves cry,
   Fed on realcrop pellets of sheepbrain skull
Because the corn that used to feed them once
   has gone to feed the cows abroad
   (not the mad ones - just the sad ones),
Mass-slaughtered on altars of MacLord
   while the Burger Crook takes space corn took.
And dark children born on roads beside it
   die blind and starving in the camel shit.

I do know the corn and these dawn circles
   always host big tractor wheels
Which gun their way across all cropswirls
   spraying Saint Monto's blue monster movie,
New Age hybrid wankenstein.
I've heard them call it Genetic Engineering.

What? Genetically engineering corn for tomorrow's
   genetically engineered male mother?
Where battery-farm plans for "egg-factory" girls
   Are all the New Age rage, big brother:
When a microchip inside your hip
   Will help us all act like each other.

But I don't know much
I don't know much
about this other thing... corn circles

But as for right now, this other thing:
Forget those two old liars with string
  who laid claim to hoaxing everything ...
I'm not saying it's definitely all a sting,
  like a pot of quids and farmers plotting;
I'm not just saying it's down to badgers rutting,
  or a persistent plasma vortex goblin,
  or the airy wiles of a flatulent Djinn.
For it just might be some Spaceship Thing.

I do know if it be a spaceship ...
Well, why would it be do you suppose
  that they would nest where our corn grows?
Hell! really of course, it's easy to see;
  just open your eyes to ET theory!
They can clearly look down
  from the big mothership,
  through little grey spores on insectoid hip:
And they see all this Corn,
  just ... sticking up ...
Well, it's there, and it's yellow,
It's a sign of luck:
Easy to mistake for the Sun maybe,
  if you were heading out of the Galaxy,
  to join the trans-Orion skyway.
And, it's far more cheap to park in the corn
than on Britain's ever-growing Highway.

But I don't know much
No I don't know much
... about corn circles

A FRIEND FROM THE STARS

North Cymru, 1980

S mall Tara is looking out of the bedroom window,
There's a sadness of sorts in endarkened eyes;
But still her face remains a glow
  in forgetfulness of ancient lies.
Wearing the toy bandage on her arm
  since daddy left and ... mummy followed;
She's playing nurses and seeming calm
  as she looks out fiercely across night sky
Which stretches far, forever high,
  shining with riches you can't deny
  last longer than those in purses.

Small Tara looks out at Venus and Mars,
  thinks of Captain Kirk and spacefilm bars.
What she wants is a real friend from the stars,
  not earthly deserters in their primitive cars;
All she wants is just a friend from the stars.
  But oh! Little Tara's no fool, she's not:
  Tomorrow, she'll settle for a parking lot.

DONGARUSALEM

Twyford Down, 1992

Well, Channel Four left them a camera
    to try to catch the best highlights;
But no-one there knew how to use it,
    or else pagans think it bites.

There were so many moments
    evading concrete house-inmates' laughs
Like evenings playing their mellifluous songs
    on home-made shaman harps;
And Sam, as thin as world democracy
    wielding the mighty axe,
Reducing titans of dead treetrunks
    to kindling size in stacks.
Between her and Stef they (almost) got me
    cured of the demon cigarettes;
The Real World talks to you up there,
    words that our race forgets.

It wasn't just about prostrating
    before the bulldozer clown,
There was a whole dimension of experience
    up there on Twyford Down.

I don't know how they did it
   (spot my inferior Arian complex!)
As they carved Pan pipes
   and discussed Stonehenge
As an ancient shrine of solstice sex ...

They didn't hold out a begging bowl
   for blood money from the State;
They were the most unsold-out of souls
   that I have seen to date.
They didn't need drugs, or pubs, or TV,
   or deodorant or tabloid scum,
And not having it didn't make them
   want to dump on anyone.

It wasn't just about upsetting
   the bullshit-dozer clown;
It was all about Real Learning
   up there on Twyford Down.

The Undead brought their oddities
  to invade our children's land.
They came, snatched human host bodies,
  possessed by a strange command
To desecrate and vandalise,
  to pillage and destroy,
From Planet Tarmach One in a Galaxy
  that has sold the keys to joy.

In days gone by we did pilgrimage
  to ancient Gods called Trees,
And now they sacrifice everything
  to the same Gods' minted leaves.

But a small tribe of resistance
  will dance firm upon this ground,
My teachers of persistence
  up there on Twyford Down.

"Will all myrrh-maids please leave the site"

THE PENTONVILLIAD

Excerpts from The Ballad of HMP Hiltonville, June 1994

When I "danced ritualistically" on Twyford Down,
  to quote the Court,
I felt an inspired sort of enlightened clown.
And as for dancing, it was news to me,
  I didn't know I was capable.
But full of cynical, sarcastic wit
  I must have been, 'cause I got four months for it.
Ironically, it sort of occurred to me
  that the last time dancing was deemed illegal
Was probably back in the good old days
  of Witch hunts, Puritans and mad Ollie Cromwell.
We've clearly progressed a very long way
Now they hire blue-meanies to lock up dancers,
  and those strange young people who go to raves
  really deserve to be arrested and jailed;
Otherwise, the Witch hunts failed.

Anyway there I was, not exactly feeling nervous,
  I knew my bottom was probably safe,
  my anal virginity not exactly at risk;
This isn't, after all, America,
  Not quite your rehabilitating Attica.

To be fair, to be fair to the Men on the Square,
  the Lodge of the furtive Orange Suspenders,
Not that I'd know if many officers there
  have joined the Governors' Club on the level,
Hotel Hiltonville did me one good turn
  as well as showing me all the works of the devil:
Three classes of Yoga a week on offer!
  Just stand on your head and you learn!
Once you finally discover it,
  you can get to do Yoga, keep splendidly fit.
Ooh! It was a wonderful, marvellous feeling,
  a real reminder of Body as Temple;
And it was the only time you saw a real woman ...
As the long weeks of idol libido dragged on
  She seemed to grow ever more beautiful,
She, the one who taught us the Yoga.
  Often dribbling cons would come in and ogle...
She'd correct our postures (I mean 'our asanas')
  with the gentlest of professional fingertips
Lots of the boys seemed to make posture-errors
  (barely retaining their base-shakti drips) ...

While there is (perchance) a singular absence
  of abductions by UFOnauts from H.M. Prisons,
Do not think there is no Lochnessian phenomenon
  to be discovered there in mundane visions:

For the eternal mystery of every cell floor,
  no matter how much you sweep and mop,
There is always green fluff, green fluff,
  green fluff stuff.
Under the mouldy bed, under buckets of slop,
  under the table, under the chair.
The rationalists argue with their usual
  pathological dogma for the unexplainable,
That all Green Fluff comes from the mattress
  - but if that were the case, if it were really true,
There'd be no mattress left at all,
  judging from this sheer mass of inexplicable
  Green Fluff manifesting wall to wall.
Unless it's just Urban Orgone residue.
It seems there can be only one possibility
  to explain it away at the end of the day:
What looks like Green Fluff, in actuality,
  is the faecal dropping of Jailhouse Ghosts:
The quasi-ectoplasmic turds
  of ever-circling phantom hosts.
It's nice to be reminded, in practicality,
  that in Hotel Hiltonville there's a Fortean fable,
For even when you hit the shower
  you can find these Ghost Turds in your navel.

21

TEARS OF JONAH

Amsterdam, April 1990

Pouring out the kettle water
  Talking silence of the other
Immaculately saddened daughter
Pretending not ... she hates her selves
Her broken, unbreakable sleeping elves
  (knows not she's Chosen)
While desperate to save all sufferers
Whales, foxes, mutoids, Mothers
Reaping rageless, the lies of lovers

Falling out the nettle sky
Her spells spring hazel runes of autumn
  to quell the fire of saddened trees
Dreamstorming new dawns
  breathed by no-one

Someone else went west to open
Gates of scorn untouched by eyes:
How I wonder why we chose
  such different paths
  on wild beasts' toes ...
This colour-changing Wolfmouse rose,
  to dream with ... no-one.

V.E. NO TREE DAY

A3 Maple Memorial Avenue, Surrey.   April 1995.
Especially for Slim (Lewis) Bradford.

They were the flower of Canadian youth
  shipped over here to fight and serve,
That we might be forever free
  of a goose-step *ein-zwei-drei* Police State.
They came in hundreds to these shores
  when our countryside still smelled of Earth,
And a thousand more colours of butterfly
  encircled flowers we see no more,
Thanks to steel and concrete gods of greyness
  raised today in the roar of progress.

They hatched from mothers' wombs wrenched sore
  to breathe a few forgotten years,
Then trembling in a vivid courage
  their chance to dance was scorched to ashes.
They lost it all, they gave up all, for the rest of us.
These were real men of flesh and blood,
Not medallions of an ancient Jesus;
That we might be forever free
  of a goose-step circus whose decree
was *ein reich* for all, or more gas chambers
  of modern roaring New Age progress.

Six hundred trees were planted for them,
   each consecrated to one of six hundred men:
Not gravestones heaped upon a pavement,
   but a living natural memorial;
A monument to their total braveness.

Six hundred sturdy maple trees,
   whose greenleafed fingers touched the sky:
And though the unborn wonder "What *were* trees?
   Mummy, *what* bygone unicorns are these?"
I must assure our tiny suns of daughters,
   trees really were quite lovely creatures;
"Possibly", as a jester said,
   "they're from a dinosaur age,
   and thus quite frightening";
"Possibly", as one soldier jested,
   "they needed to go as a danger to lightning!"
With their breezy whispers rippling under stars.
But who could deny for the sake of progress,
   they *had* to go -
They terrorised all passing cars.

So when the Maple Avenue was finally felled,
    ripped down like british credibility,
So that no more could their wet, green, natural smells
    violate our windscreen-shielded sanctity,
It was conspicuous that five or six
    full riot vans of mocking helmets
Should form a two-mile wall of armour
    to keep at bay the Progress Harmer:
That unconsulted local resident
    who desperately wanted the Trees to stay,
At least for five more weeks until
    the Canadian Veteran Survivors came
To remember their comrades on VE Day.

Do I detect an ironic sniff of Fate
    that the New World Order's brave Police State
Forms its wall of leather-booted armour
    to protect the modern would-be men
Who rip down the final Monument
    to those who died at barely adult age
To stop the rise of a Police State's rage?

FAIR-MINDED MAN

Jesmond Dene protest camp, Newcastle, Summer 1993

I'm a fair-minded man
   who'll look at all angles.
I never condemn
   before I know all the handles.
I mean, even the rapist
   may have been led too far
By the eight-year-old victim
   who isn't always an angel.
And I dig a big bulldozer
   which turns fields into hell,
But put one scratch on my car
   and I'll kill you as well.

THE ARCHITECTS OF ANNIHILATION

G8 Summit, Birmingham, May 1998

We gathered in the house of the holy Lamb
   to peacefully protest the deaths of children.
And many there were in the holy Lamb's place,
A great many politicised Christians.

Starving Children in Africa:
"Cancel the third World debt!" we said
   (or asked, or politely requested, or begged).
It is a sick joke, after all:
They owe us nothing, these starving children.
We took their land, their minerals,
   their resources, their petrochemicals.
We took their DNA and left a bible;
We gave them flu and AIDS, *we're* liable.
And now each unborn, starving child
   owes Big Brother nearly three hundred dollars;
And not to complain leaves *us* defiled,
   sweating under wealthy, starched white collars.

We gathered in the house of the holy Lamb,
   oblivious to the fact he's a holy Pig
In the eyes of the Papua New Guinea tribe
   whose bible version calls him the Pig of God,

On account of the fact they have no lambs,
   only pigs, which might seem slightly odd.
I do not say this to be blasphemous:
   He *is* Holy Pig to them, not us.

And many there were who spoke to us,
   most eloquently, those who cared.
There were black women, black men,
   white women, white men,
An African and an Indian.
It was great to know so many cared.

And when they spoke, their heartbeats filled
   the world of the house of the holy Pig.
Their sincerity and integrity, fully declared
   the voices of small people, almightily big.
We gathered in the house of the holy Pig
   as well-behaved as the Lamb would bid.
And then I smelled $atan's foetid armpit
   and looked around, but no-one else did.
Bloated with camera-lit ego, the Reptile entered,
   a monstrous politician from the Id:
They're doing all they possibly could
   to address the problem in fifty years' time;
And if they didn't, then someone would,
   after concealment of the next sex-crime.

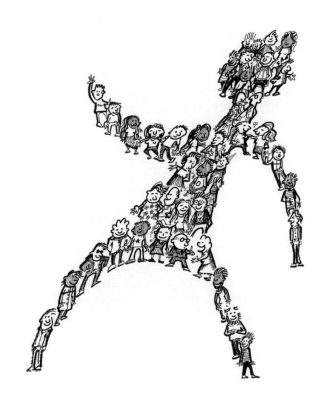

Quick! Slash state aid for single mothers,
 and single fathers, and disabled others,
While urging us all to try to believe
 they want to help starving Black sisters and brothers.

Beware that unelected, ruling global elite
 which dictates who will be new 'leader' or King.
I want to help reveal to the sheep,
 the secret truths behind election-winning.
Those good, caring people blind in their sleep
 who really don't want sick babies to die,
Applauded the Reptile and made my flesh creep
 in the house of the holy Lamb's pie in the sky.

But no hero me, in the crowd of the Thousands,
 and thousands there were in the house of the Pig.
I too kept as silent as death in sheep-land,
 my anger consigned to a bottomless pit.
My small voice did not grow almightily big ...
 but I can understand the instinct to demand
That the Reptile and her sick lord
 should roast on a spit.
They masticate our 'Third' World neighbours
 in a Holocaust of enforced starvation,
While our silent voices still permit
 the architects of annihilation.

STAY (AS LUSH WOODS SHOULD)

Somerset, July 1998

Go now... wander through the lush wood;
Leave your eyes behind in silence,
Leave your eyes to blind my violence.
Darkest eyes, like trees at midnight,
Fill the skies and soar in cloudflight.

Go now... disappear in bright reign.
Held you very quick and briefly;
And in that moment... eternity.
Long dark hair like wild worn sighs;
Morning springs and eats the midnight,
Loneliness burns red with starlight.

No "love", no, but what a feeling;
Held you close... next day you're leaving,
Wanted you for one more evening,
Washed my tongue in rivers deepening...
The river closed up wounds of evening war.

No mind... just the silent sometime.
Watched you go. Pretend I'm not watching.

Touched the end of hope's joke winning,
Tonguewash over, head still spinning more.
What do you feel? What is the feeling?
What is real is not the real thing.
Many wars ago you're dreaming,
Dreams I lost while still believing
There was something worth believing for.

Was there ever one who touched you,
Who gave a promise that you rushed to?
Was there ever one for whom you died?
Are your eyes of urban coldness
Jewel-swept with shamanic oldness?
What *vast* secrets do those jewels hide?
You made it known you're not one of these
Who stones the one who believes, believes
In the last of the world's hushed living trees
    That were once our friends for centuries.

Go now...
Wander through the lush wood
... that we hope will stay
As lush woods should.

TIME (THE REAL STORY)

Solsbury Hill protest camp, Bath, August 1994

There's a strangled Clown
    lying in the road.
They tell me he's called Time.

I'd have killed the prankster
    long ago.
I hate his pantomime.

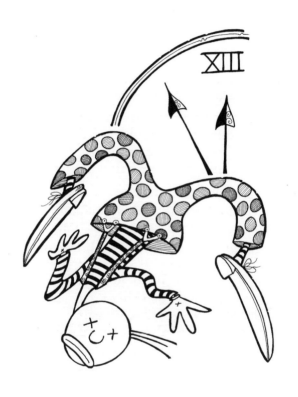

WARSZAWA SNAPS

Poland, January 1993

They've brought MuckDonalds to new Warsaw.
They've bought the neon light eyesore.
They've got the soldiers in stately grey
  fooling around in a playful way,
    down an alley with a Kalashnikov;
I like your manliness, Herr Jerkov.

They've got bright children in very tall blocks ...
They have old Warszawa's few hologram snapshots,
Now rebuilt since the age of bomb-drops
  of the fashionable dance-rage of goosestep cyclops.
They used to have so many trees
  they could fell each one for just $\frac{1}{2}$p.
Plus of course, the familiar share
  of young Madonnas with dark hair,
Braving ancient snowfalls with the Baby.
I'm still too scared to step out alone
  in some of those places where the Truth comes home.

Well, I found the heights of the chrome delights
  of the New One World Government embassy,
Not to mention the spermshop sights
  and the glitter of Rainforest burgery.

I found the bright lights, furshop pavilion
  and new age banks of pseudo-London;
But I didn't find Warsaw, only Caesar's invasion.

Oh, and I found the beggars, the darkeyed Women
  clutching tiny kids with a glazed expression,
Who know they're now in the Land of Progress
  since the applauded death of socialism,
But who wonder why they can't afford
  to feed their kids in this new prison.
Communalism was the people's re-evolution,
  that Caesar hijacked with the bolsheviks.
It doesn't appear we're mature enough for it,
  drowned in the all too familiar sea
Of all-too-readily over-believed
  unquestioned pseudo-history:
Which poor mothers know is hardly surprising,
  born from the sewer of a few rich men,
Who want to make your heart embrace
  the greater glories of their kingdom ...
One always lost at the same expense:

A small green planet in outer space,
  and all your born and unborn Children.

MOONGATE

Zeta Reticuli, March 1999

From days of horse and cart, so soon,
  they tell us 'man' walked on the Moon;
But they forgot to add a movie tune,
  and every decent movie has one.
How did they cope with Space Radiation?
How did they fool the global nation?
Were we all so desperate for celebration?
Vast moonscapes lit by electric sun.

The photographs look really good,
  as good as lunar snapshots should;
As real as Star Trek ever could:
And to the Moon we've gone ...
To boldly go where no film studio
  has ever gone for a classic show -
So few there were who'd ever know
  they got the camera shadows wrong.

I guess it was the thought that counted,
  and not the film sets that they mounted:
And not the stars they couldn't fake,
  which they omitted from the final take,
So that astronomers couldn't calculate
  it was filmed on Earth and not in Heaven.

I guess it was the hope, the dream
    that matters more than NASA's scheme
To fool us all - more than we've ever been,
With the greatest monochrome movie scene.
One small step for a man, we're told,
    one giant leap for mass mind control:
It's visions like these we *want* to hold;
They gained the Moon and lost their souls.

But one day maybe, when we know how
    to live on Earth right here and now,
Perhaps we might then be allowed
    to really land upon the Moon.
When all Earth's starving children eat,
    and that unelected crazed elite
Who guide all puppet leader-sheep
    through bottomless pits of ancient sleep,
Are banished in supreme defeat
    (and may that day reign soon):
We might just then be free to go
    beyond Apollo's old theatre show,
And really walk with smiles aglow
    upon our unpolluted Moon.

PRAYER TO AVALONIA

Avalon, Isle of Apples, March 1998

I bless the Organic Cider Goddess!
   I serve her with my life.
My hobbies are consumption
   and pure oddness,
And all else is just strife.
But still I serve the Goddess
   and the cup that never empties;
Oh Avalonia! Your sweet breasts
   drip the medicine of orchards plenty.
Oh amber-nectared Apple Goddess,
   your eyes rich with drunken benediction:
I offer my liver as a sacrifice,
   to bless you with a drooped mid-section.

I freely give gutspill to the Earth,
   to fertilize your pear-shaped flowers.
I thank you for a full belly's worth
   and commune with you for many hours,
In holy devotional self-liquidation
   that fills me with divine sensation.

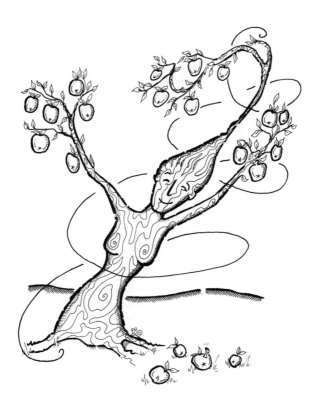

Never leave me, Apple-Goddess,
   with your earth-moving caress...
You make the walls spin round and round.
Only a real Goddess can do that.
You alter minds faster than the speed of sound,
   and even taste great when you're flat.

It was a woman who drove me unto you,
   and I never had the courtesy to thank her.
She drove me to your arms, and threw
   Me unto thee, shouting "What a Plonker!"
Oh wet-lipped, apple-scented Goddess,
   fill me with Grail Elixir Cider...
Thrill me with your spin vortex
   and let me sleep inside her.

Tell me Jesus, Jesus, could it be true?
Is this a bible coverup
   which others have seen through?
Was it good *Cider* in the wedding cup
   You turned the water into?

CAN ORPHANS KNOW THEIR PARENTS?

Somerset crop circle, June 1998

O h! Look up mummy, in the sky!
    That strange cloud's something in disguise;
A great fireball spitting many coloured flames,
  known by a thousand ancient names,
Where lights that pose as starship and faerie
  dance the trance of unknown reality:
And alone, at night, can be quite scary
  in the Dark that drowns all triviality.

I believe in the Faeries! I've seen their miracles!
I know that *they* can hoax the circles!
These temples come like thieves by night
  as signs and wonders in the land;
Enchanted songs that fools must fight
  to deny what we can't understand.
Kali-Isis, like the Kraken, wakes
  and erupts volcanoes in her pain;
Our Atlantis falls beneath earthquakes.
We'll never be the same again.

AMERICA! I LOVE YOU

Somerset, May 1999

Twenty-six Long Years for stealing a biscuit!
   Has Uncle Sam gone barking mad,
 or is the Judge just slightly twisted?
Of course not! The prisoner should be a Real Man,
   serving his country, dropping bombs
   on all Sam's enemies' mums and children!
Not walking around biscuit-stealing ...
Yes, I guess I understand the Judge's feeling
   (even though my head's still reeling).

"Three strikes and you're Out"
   was the cocaine President's warning shout
   (if you're black and poor and hungry with it):
I really hope it was a tasty biscuit,
   and he got to eat every crumb of it;
Though he couldn't have done -
   That would be the evidence gone!
Was it a double-cream chocolate-topped
   superdigestive?
No, luckily it was just a stale plain cookie:
   or else Sam must double the sentence,
                              surely ...